Original title:
Lost and Found

Copyright © 2024 Swan Charm
All rights reserved.

Author: Kene Elistrand
ISBN HARDBACK: 978-9916-79-230-8
ISBN PAPERBACK: 978-9916-79-231-5
ISBN EBOOK: 978-9916-79-232-2

From Ashes to Altar

From ashes we rise, in fervent prayer,
Hearts entwined in hope, seeking the rare.
In trials we find, the strength to stand,
A faithful spirit, held in His hand.

On altars of grace, our burdens laid,
In the warmth of love, our fears soon fade.
With every tear, a promise made,
In the light of faith, our path is paved.

The flames may roar, but faith ignites,
Through darkest nights, the soul alights.
Embrace the fire, let it consume,
For from the blaze, new life will bloom.

Hidden Blessings in the Wilderness

In wilderness vast, His whispers flow,
Through tangled roots, His secrets grow.
Amongst the thorns, we learn to see,
Hidden blessings, wild and free.

The path may twist, the shadows loom,
Yet faith will shine, dispelling gloom.
With every trial, lessons unfold,
A treasure trove, more precious than gold.

In quiet moments, the heart will hear,
The gentle call, that draws us near.
Amidst the trials, there lies a song,
A melody sweet, where we belong.

The Return of the Wandering Spirit

O wandering spirit, lost in the night,
Return to the fold, seek the guiding light.
Through valleys deep, and mountains high,
In every breath, hear the Spirit's sigh.

With every step, redemption near,
Forgive the past, cast away fear.
In the arms of grace, you'll find your rest,
A journey home, you are truly blessed.

The call of love, it echoes loud,
Through every storm, you rise unbowed.
In softened hearts, the truth ignites,
The bridled soul, restored in His light.

Seraphim and Shadows

In realms above, the seraphim sing,
With voices pure, they praise the King.
Yet shadows linger, whispering lies,
A battle waged, beneath the skies.

With wings of fire, they guard the way,
Bringing hope's dawn, to the break of day.
In light's embrace, shadows take flight,
Through faith and love, we embrace the night.

With every prayer, the veil grows thin,
Seraphim's glow, we invite within.
In the heart's temple, let peace reside,
For in His presence, fear will subside.

The Silent Reverie of Forsaken Joy

In shadows deep where sorrows cling,
A heart once bright, now lost its zing.
Silent prayers in the night unfurl,
Echoes of joy in a muted whirl.

The whispers fade, like dust in air,
Memories of laughter, a silent prayer.
Yet in the stillness, hope may rise,
A flicker of light in the darkened skies.

Forsaken dreams, they wander still,
Seeking a path, a gentle will.
In reverie's grasp, we find our way,
From shadows cast to a brighter day.

With each tear shed, a lesson learned,
From ashes bleak, a passion burned.
The silent reverie, a gift bestowed,
In the heart's embrace, our spirits flowed.

From Desolation to Divine Light

In barren lands where hope seems lost,
A weary soul pays such a cost.
Yet from the depths, a whisper calls,
A promise waiting beyond the walls.

From desolation, seeds take flight,
Nurtured by faith, blossoming bright.
Through trials faced and shadows past,
A journey forged, our hearts steadfast.

In quiet moments, divine grace flows,
Turning the dark where the river goes.
Finding solace in every sigh,
Transforming pain to dreams that fly.

The light shall break through tempest's might,
Guiding souls in the silent night.
From ashes pure, new life will grow,
In every heart, His love shall show.

The Remnants of Yesterday's Reverence

In echoes soft of days gone by,
The remnants hum like a sacred sigh.
Reverence lost in the passage of time,
Yet grace, like a river, continues to climb.

In memories bright, the spirit resides,
Through trials endured, the faith abides.
With every shadow that dances near,
We reach for the light, and the dawn draws near.

Whispers of wisdom from ages old,
Stories of love in their hands to hold.
In every pulse, a call to be free,
The remnants beckon, come follow me.

As seasons change, and moments fade,
In reverence found, the heart is laid.
Echoes of yesterday still sing true,
In every breath, His love shines through.

A Tapestry of Lost Whispers

In threads of gold, the whispers weave,
A tapestry formed of dreams we leave.
Lost in the fabric of time's embrace,
Each stitch a story, each line a grace.

From silent corners the voices rise,
Carrying hopes to the starlit skies.
In every fiber, a tale unfolds,
Of love and joy, of the brave and bold.

The quiet echoes of what was known,
In shadows cast, the seeds are sown.
A prayer in the night, a promise made,
In the heart's realm, we find our aid.

With tapestry rich in hues divine,
We gather strength, through love we bind.
Whispers of faith in each gentle thread,
Together we weave, where angels tread.

Beneath the Archway of Hope

Beneath the archway, we stand in grace,
Guided by light in a sacred space.
With whispers of faith, our spirits rise,
Embraced by love that never dies.

In trials faced, we seek the way,
Each moment counts in the light of day.
The heart finds peace, the soul takes flight,
In the shadowed path, we find the light.

With every prayer, we stitch the seams,
Of dreams entwined in celestial beams.
The archway wide, our journey unfolds,
In every heartbeat, a story told.

Together we walk on this hallowed ground,
In unity lost, yet ever found.
A tapestry woven of joy and strife,
Beneath the archway, we discover life.

So gather close, let the echoes ring,
Through love's embrace, our spirits sing.
Beneath the archway, we stand secure,
In the arms of grace, we find our cure.

A Chronicle of the Unremembered

In shadows deep where silence dwells,
Lies a tale that time compels.
Echoes of prayers, in whispers fade,
A chronicle lost, yet still conveyed.

Forgotten faces, a silent creed,
In every heart, a planted seed.
Memories linger, like dreams in flight,
A tapestry woven in the night.

Though time erases, love still remains,
In every tear, in every pain.
The unremembered, reach for the divine,
In devotion pure, our souls entwine.

Through ancient lines, the stories flow,
Of faith unyielding, through highs and lows.
In the book of life, each heart will find,
The sacred truths that forever bind.

A blessing bestowed on those unknown,
In every heartbeat, we are not alone.
In the darkness fades, the light shall rise,
A chronicle sings beneath the skies.

The Blessing of the Wayward Heart

In wandering paths, the wayward roam,
Seeking solace far from home.
Yet every step, though lost it seems,
Carries a spark of sacred dreams.

The heart may falter, the spirit stray,
Yet grace awaits at the break of day.
Each stumble holds a lesson deep,
In the wayward journey, find the leap.

With tears as prayers, they cleanse the soul,
In moments dark, they become whole.
Each heartbeat echoes the call of grace,
As the wayward find their rightful place.

Through trials fierce, and shadows cast,
The blessing shines, a light steadfast.
In every struggle, a purpose found,
The wayward heart, forever unbound.

So walk with courage, embrace the fight,
In wanderings wild, discover the light.
For grace extends to souls that roam,
In the wayward heart, we find our home.

Reflections from the Forgotten Pool

In the stillness of twilight's embrace,
Lies a forgotten pool, a sacred space.
Mirrored water holds our tales unseen,
Reflecting the hearts that once had been.

In ripples soft, the past reveals,
Secrets whispered, the soul it heals.
The quietude beckons a gentle sigh,
In the depths we find the reasons why.

With every glance, the memories surge,
In sacred waters, our spirits merge.
Tears may fall, yet blessings flow,
From the forgotten, new life will grow.

The moonlight dances upon the shore,
Awakening dreams we can't ignore.
In tranquil depths, the truth will bloom,
Reflections gather, dispelling the gloom.

So let us pause, and drink it in,
The wisdom found in where we've been.
In the forgotten pool, we weave our fate,
From stillness stirs, a love so great.

The Unseen Path of Grace

In shadows deep, His light shines bright,
Guiding hearts through the endless night.
With gentle whispers, faith does grow,
Upon the path where graces flow.

Each step we take, a sacred dance,
In trials faced, we find our chance.
With open hearts, we seek His face,
On the unseen path of grace.

Through valleys low and mountains high,
The spirit lifts, we touch the sky.
In every tear, a purpose found,
In love's embrace, our souls unbound.

As burdens shift, and burdens yield,
Our hearts are healed, our wounds concealed.
Through faith we stand, though storms may rage,
We walk the road, the unturned page.

With every dawn, He bids us rise,
In morning light, hope never dies.
For in the dark, His promise gleams,
A testament to all our dreams.

Revelations Amidst the Ruins

In crumbled walls, the truth reveals,
A light that breaks, a heart that heals.
Amongst the ashes, whispers call,
To rise, to learn, to love it all.

The skies may weep, the earth may quake,
Yet from the dust, new life we make.
In every ruin, a grace bestowed,
To find the strength in what erodes.

With every sigh, a prayer is sent,
In brokenness, our spirits blend.
From shattered dreams, we seek to find,
The sacred threads that bind mankind.

In darkness, sparks of hope ignite,
With every step, we claim the light.
Through struggles faced, our souls unite,
In revelations, pure and bright.

So here we stand, amidst the fall,
With faith as strong, it conquers all.
For in each ruin, we understand,
God's hand restores this weary land.

Ascending from the Abyss

From depths so dark, a cry ascends,
A plea for light, where silence bends.
Yet in the void, a spark ignites,
Through faith we climb to greater heights.

The weight of doubt, a heavy chain,
But love ignites and breaks the pain.
With every heartbeat, hope resounds,
In trials faced, our strength abounds.

A hand reaches down from above,
To lift us high, a gift of love.
In every fall, we rise anew,
With wings of faith, we pierce the blue.

As storms may rage, and shadows loom,
Our spirits soar, dispelling gloom.
For in the abyss, we find our worth,
In grace bestowed, we are rebirthed.

So onward still, we seek the light,
With hearts aglow, we share the fight.
For from the depths, we rise and sing,
In His embrace, we have all things.

The Pilgrimage of Broken Promises

Through winding paths of shattered dreams,
We walk the road, or so it seems.
Yet in the gaps of hopes once held,
The heart finds strength, and spirit swelled.

Each promise made, a seed we plant,
Though some take flight, others recant.
In every step of doubt and grace,
We find the truth in this sacred space.

For every tear, a lesson learned,
In broken vows, our hearts have burned.
Yet from the ashes, faith will rise,
With eyes aflame, we seek the skies.

So let us walk with humble hearts,
Embrace the pain that love imparts.
For on this path, though fraught with loss,
We bear the cross, no matter the cost.

Through every trial, we are made whole,
A journey blessed, a destined goal.
In every promise that slips away,
Hope lights the dawn of a new day.

The Echoes of Eden

In the garden of grace, where blessings bloom,
Angels whisper softly, dispelling gloom.
Fruit of wisdom, in the cool, calm air,
Eden's whispers echo, a divine prayer.

Beneath the ancient trees, shadows dance,
In their presence, we find our chance.
With every step, the path unfolds,
Stories of love in the silence told.

Where rivers flow with the sweetest song,
In harmony with heaven, we belong.
The laughter of children, pure and fair,
In Eden's embrace, we wander there.

Yet the shadows deepen, hearts may stray,
Longing for the light, we seek the way.
In the echoes of Eden, we yearn to find,
The grace that transcends both space and time.

Grains of Truth in the Dust

In the quiet corners where shadows throng,
Lie the grains of truth, simple yet strong.
Footprints of the faithful, etched in dust,
In each sacred journey, we place our trust.

Wisdom whispers softly through the years,
Collecting our sorrow, our joys, our fears.
Every tear and laughter, a part of the tale,
In the tapestry woven, love will prevail.

Nature sings of miracle, night and day,
In the rhythms of life, we find our way.
A world painted with strokes of divine light,
Turning darkness to dawn, wrong into right.

Hands that toil with humility's grace,
Gather the dust in each sacred place.
Together we rise, with spirits anew,
In the grains of truth, our hearts beat true.

Through the Veil of Forgotten Dreams

Beyond the veil where daylight fades,
Lie the dreams we've lost in dark cascades.
Fleeting visions wander, yet hope still glows,
In the silence of night, the spirit knows.

Whispers of the past, they softly call,
Each yearning heart bears burdens small.
Memories of laughter, echoes of grace,
In the canvas of time, we find our place.

Threads of faith interwoven tight,
Mending the fabric of day and night.
Through shadows, we wander, searching for light,
Forging new paths, breaking the night.

In forgotten dreams, the soul takes flight,
With wings that shimmer in the twilight.
Through the veil, we seek, we believe,
In the dawn of new hope, we shall achieve.

A Prayer for the Wayward Soul

In the depth of night, where shadows creep,
A prayer rises softly, gentle as sleep.
For those who wander, lost and alone,
May the light of compassion lead them home.

With every heartbeat, love begins to swell,
Creating a bridge where memories dwell.
In the arms of mercy, find your rest,
In the aching heart, be fully blessed.

Through storms of sorrow, through trials vast,
May strength be found in the shadows cast.
In the darkest hours, hope still gleams,
Guiding wayward souls toward their dreams.

With every tear that finds its way,
A promise endures, to light the way.
In the embrace of faith, we stand tall,
A prayer for the wayward, loved by all.

The Silent Dawn of Understanding

In stillness we seek the light,
Awakening hearts in the night.
Whispers of truth softly descend,
Guiding our souls to the end.

With each sigh, wisdom is born,
Beneath the veil of the morn.
Eyes closed, yet visions appear,
In silence, we hold what is dear.

The dawn breaks with a gentle grace,
Illuminating every face.
In unity, we find our way,
Together at the break of day.

Through trials, the spirit will soar,
Embracing what we've learned before.
In every struggle, we trust the plan,
For understanding is the essence of man.

With faith, we walk the sacred ground,
In the hush, true peace is found.
The silent dawn, a precious gift,
Through love and understanding, our spirits lift.

The Wings of Forgotten Prayers

In the shadows where hope resides,
Wings unfold as the spirit guides.
Forgotten whispers, cradled tight,
Lifted heavensward, out of sight.

Echoes of love in the still of night,
Restoration born from sacred light.
Each prayer a breath, soft and clear,
Carried forth, to those we hold dear.

In silent chambers where hearts ignite,
Our faith takes flight, a beautiful sight.
No longer bound by earthly ties,
The wings of prayers, they strive and rise.

From depths of sorrow, beauty grows,
As every heart in harmony flows.
Together we soar, unconfined,
As love's embrace leaves doubts behind.

In the tapestry of the divine,
Each prayer a thread, we intertwine.
With grateful hearts, we all ascend,
In shadows cast, our souls will mend.

A Dance with the Shadows of Legacy

In the twilight, shadows play,
Echoes of those who've gone away.
We gather strength from their refrain,
In a dance of joy, amidst the pain.

Legacy whispers through the breeze,
Carrying tales among the trees.
Every step, a memory spun,
In the light of those who've overcome.

The rhythm of life, in sync we move,
Bound by the love that we will prove.
In a waltz of grace, let hearts connect,
As we honor all that we reflect.

Each shadow a guide, subtle, wise,
Illuminating truths as time flies.
In our dance, their spirits revive,
Through every heartbeat, they truly survive.

Together we twirl, hand in hand,
Finding solace in this sacred land.
For every legacy holds a spark,
Illuminating paths in the dark.

The Gathering of Shattered Halos

Beneath the stars, we take our stand,
Gathering pieces, hand in hand.
Shattered halos, broken dreams,
In unity, hope always redeems.

Each fragment tells a tale of grace,
A journey of love in this sacred space.
Through cracks, the light begins to flow,
An orchestra of healing will grow.

In the embrace of the night sky,
We lift our voices; spirits fly.
For every scar reveals the light,
In shadows deep, we find our sight.

With every heart, we weave anew,
A tapestry of courage, pure and true.
Gathered now, we rise above,
In shattered pieces, we find love.

Together we shine, luminous and bright,
Guided by the stars in the night.
In every gathering, solace we seek,
With shattered halos, we are unique.

The Harvest of the Wayward Seed

In fields where shadows softly creep,
A wayward seed, its promise deep.
By gentle hands, the soil is stirred,
Awakening hope in silent word.

Beneath the sun's warm, loving rays,
It finds its strength in winding ways.
While storms may seek to tear it down,
The heart of faith will wear the crown.

With whispered prayers, the farmer toils,
Nurturing dreams in sacred soils.
For every loss, a lesson learned,
In every heart, the yearning burned.

As seasons change and times go by,
The harvest blooms beneath the sky.
The wayward seed, once lost and lone,
Now yields a bounty all its own.

From darkest nights and trials brief,
Springs forth a joy beyond all grief.
In every grain, a story's seed,
The world transforms through love's great need.

Whispers of the Forgotten

Among the ruins, shadows play,
Silent echoes of yesterday.
The whispers call from deeper wells,
A tapestry of untold bells.

Lost in time's relentless flow,
Forgotten souls, where do they go?
Each voice a thread, each tear a sign,
Binding us in love divine.

In quiet corners, faith awakes,
A flicker of hope, the heart it stakes.
For those unseen, let courage rise,
In every soul, a promise lies.

Embracing all, both meek and bold,
Stories of ancient truths unfold.
Through whispered prayers, we find our way,
Illuminating the dawn of day.

As night retreats, we lift our glance,
United in this sacred dance.
The forgotten rise in light's embrace,
Finding joy in love's vast space.

Echoes of the Wanderer's Heart

Upon the road, the wanderer treads,
With weary shoes and dreams unsaid.
Each step a prayer, each mile a plea,
In search of peace, to set him free.

Through valleys low and mountains high,
The heart seeks truth beneath the sky.
In distant lands where shadows play,
The light of love will guide the way.

Voices murmur in the breeze,
Carried forth by ancient trees.
Each echo sings of hope's embrace,
In every heart, a sacred space.

The journey bends, yet never ends,
With every turn, the spirit mends.
For in the quest, the soul finds grace,
A wanderer's heart shall know its place.

At sunset's glow, horizons call,
To every rise, there's yet a fall.
But in each heartbeat, wisdom grows,
The echoes whisper love bestows.

The Relic of Grace

In hallowed halls where sunlight beams,
Lie relics wrapped in prayerful dreams.
Touched by hands both young and old,
   Stories of grace in silence told.

The weight of time can feel so vast,
Yet moments linger, shadows cast.
Each relic holds a sacred trace,
Of love divine, the gift of grace.

In quiet reverence, we draw near,
With thankful hearts, we hold what's dear.
A melody, soft as a sigh,
Reminds us how the spirit flies.

Through trials faced and burdens borne,
The relic shines, the heart reborn.
For every tear, a jewel rare,
In every story, God's tender care.

Let us embrace what time reveals,
In every relic, truth that heals.
With open hearts, we seek the face,
Of love eternal, the relic of grace.

The Heart's Uncharted Terrain

In silence deep, where shadows dwell,
The heart's vast field begins to swell.
With faith as guide, we seek to roam,
In sacred whispers, we find our home.

Each step we take, a prayer unfolds,
In warmth of light, our truth beholds.
Through valleys low, and mountains high,
The spirit's map, the soul's reply.

In every ache, a lesson learned,
In trials faced, a flame discerned.
With every heartbeat, grace we find,
Navigating pathways, love intertwined.

When doubt surrounds, and shadows creep,
In trust we stand, our burdens keep.
With every breath, a sacred trust,
In the heart's terrain, we move, we must.

To love unbound, to seek the Divine,
In every moment, by design.
Together we walk, hand in hand,
In the heart's embrace, forever stand.

Revelations from the Abyss

From depths unknown, a voice does rise,
In darkness deep, the spirit flies.
A call to hearts, who dare to hear,
In silence deep, the truth draws near.

Emerging from the shadows bleak,
An echo stirs, as spirits speak.
In trials faced, the wisdom grows,
Revelations found where courage flows.

In every tear, a story told,
In every sorrow, courage bold.
Through pain we learn, through loss we gain,
In depths of love, we break the chain.

With faith as armor, we will tread,
Through paths of darkness, where angels lead.
With open hearts, the truth embraced,
In the abyss, we find our grace.

So shine the light, in shadows cast,
With every step, the die is cast.
In revelations, our souls unite,
From the abyss, we rise in light.

The Spirit in the Wilderness

In wild expanse, where nature breathes,
The spirit roams, the heart believes.
Amidst the trees, so tall and wise,
We seek the truth, beneath the skies.

With gentle wind, our souls take flight,
In whispered prayers, we find our light.
Through rugged paths, the journey's clear,
In wilderness vast, we draw so near.

A song of hope fills every space,
In nature's song, we find our grace.
Each rustling leaf, a sacred sound,
In every step, the love we've found.

To walk in faith, through thorns and bloom,
In every shadow, the spirit's loom.
With open eyes, we see the way,
In wilderness grand, the dawn of day.

Together we tread, hand in hand,
In spirit strong, our dreams expand.
In wild embrace, we find our home,
In realms of peace, we freely roam.

Mended by the Sacred Light

In weary hearts, the light will shine,
With gentle touch, the love divine.
In broken dreams, hope starts to gleam,
Mended souls, in the spirit's beam.

Through darkest nights, when shadows play,
The sacred light will show the way.
With every crack, a story told,
In healing warmth, the heart grows bold.

In quiet moments, grace unfolds,
With every hug, and hands to hold.
As dawn arrives, the shadows flee,
In sacred light, we're meant to be.

A tapestry of love and care,
In every stitch, the spirit's share.
Mended by hands, both kind and true,
In light embraced, we start anew.

With every step, we walk in hope,
In trials faced, we learn to cope.
Together we rise, our hearts in flight,
In love's embrace, we're mended right.

Fragments of Divine Memory

In whispers soft, the past unfolds,
The echoes of souls, in light and gold.
Each moment lingers, a sacred thread,
We weave our stories, where angels tread.

In quiet hours, the heart will yearn,
For glimpses of grace, from which we learn.
The fragments dance, in twilight's gleam,
A tapestry woven, a holy dream.

Through trials faced, the spirit grows,
In valleys low, the love bestows.
With every tear, a blessing sown,
In the silent depths, we're never alone.

As stars align, our paths will meet,
In divine moments, we feel complete.
The memories linger, soft as prayer,
With faith as our guide, we rise from despair.

In fragments whole, we find our place,
In every heartbeat, we glimpse His grace.
Together we journey, hand in hand,
In the garden of life, where love will stand.

In Search of the Sacred Path

In golden dawn, where shadows creep,
We wander forth, our promise deep.
With hearts aflame, we seek the truth,
In every step, the light of youth.

With whispered prayers, we seek the way,
Through tangled woods, where hopes can sway.
Each winding road, a lesson learned,
The sacred fire within us burned.

In quiet moments, we pause and see,
The beauty found in simplicity.
A path adorned with grace and love,
As sacred winds push dreams above.

Through storm and strife, we hold on tight,
Guided by faith, through darkest night.
The sacred path reveals its charm,
Embracing us with open arms.

In every heartbeat, the truth will shine,
A melody sweet, divine design.
Together we walk, hand in hand,
Towards the horizon, where hopes expand.

Beneath the Veil of Shadows

Beneath the veil, the silence speaks,
Where hidden hopes and sorrow leaks.
In shadowed corners, faith still glows,
A gentle whisper, where love bestows.

In darkest nights, the soul ignites,
Through trials faced, the spirit fights.
With every tear, a lesson learned,
In every heart, a flame returned.

The shadows dance, a fleeting guise,
As we search for truth behind closed eyes.
In every heartbeat, a chance to heal,
For light will break, and pain will peel.

In the quiet hush, we find our peace,
Through every doubt, our fears release.
Beneath the veil, we rise and stand,
Guided by grace, we'll understand.

In unity, we lift the shroud,
With voices raised, in praise we're loud.
Beneath the veil of shadows cast,
Our faith will guide us, strong and steadfast.

The Sunlit Shard

In morning's light, a shard does gleam,
A promise woven, a sacred dream.
With every dawn, the world awakes,
To harvest gifts that love creates.

Through rustling leaves, the whispers flow,
In sunlit rays, our spirits grow.
Each precious moment, a glimpse of grace,
Reflection of truth, in time and space.

In unity's light, we stand as one,
As hope ignites, like stars undone.
The sunlit shard holds stories bright,
Of love embraced, dispelling night.

With every smile, the world expands,
In giving freely, we join our hands.
Together we shine, a beacon pure,
In every heart, the love will assure.

In sunlit choruses, we find our song,
With every note, we all belong.
In the warmth of love, we shall transcend,
The sunlit shard, our hearts will mend.

The Fountain of Distant Echoes

In prayerful whispers, waters flow,
Eternal truths like rivers glow.
From distant shores, the echoes call,
In sacred silence, we find our all.

Beneath the stars, the heavens weave,
A tapestry of hopes we cleave.
Each droplet sings of love and grace,
In every heart, a sacred space.

The fountain springs, refreshing hearts,
As faith ignites and doubt departs.
Through trials faced, we rise anew,
In unity, our spirits grew.

With every sip, the spirit soars,
Beyond the gates of worldly doors.
In tranquil depths, our souls unite,
Beneath the moon's soft, guiding light.

The echoes dance in twilight's glow,
A promise kept in ebb and flow.
Revealing paths where we must tread,
With gratitude, our souls are fed.

The Awakening of Silent Promises

In the stillness, whispers rise,
Silent vows beneath the skies.
Hearts aligned in sacred trust,
Awakening ashes back to dust.

Each promise spoken, softly clear,
Carried forth by faith, not fear.
In shadows deep, we shall not wane,
For love's pure light will break the chain.

Through trials faced and darkness met,
Our spirits vow and never forget.
From silent depths, the strength we find,
In unity, we're redefined.

The dawn approaches, bright and warm,
With every sunrise, hearts transform.
Eclipsing doubt, our voices blend,
In faith we journey, hand in hand.

As petals bloom, the promise grows,
In grace we rise, the spirit knows.
Awake, arise, let love convene,
In every moment, felt and seen.

A Map To the Unseen Realms

With ink of light, the map unfolds,
Through ancient tales, the truth beholds.
In sacred symbols carved with care,
We journey forth beyond despair.

Each path reveals a deeper sight,
The unseen realms, our guiding light.
In prayers whispered like soft rain,
Our spirits soar, and hope remains.

From valleys low to mountains high,
The map leads forth beneath the sky.
With every step, the heart awakes,
In sharing love, the journey makes.

The horizon glows with golden grace,
In every challenge, we embrace.
With trust, we seek what lies ahead,
In faith, we find the path we tread.

So take this map, and learn to see,
The unseen realms, our destiny.
For every soul, the journey's meant,
In joyous peace, our lives are spent.

Embracing the Echo of Absence

In silent nights, a whisper breathes,
The echo of absence, truth that cleaves.
Each gentlest sigh, a memory's grace,
In depths of loss, we find our place.

With every heartbeat, love remains,
A symphony played on fragile strains.
Though shadows cast where light once shone,
In absence felt, our spirits grown.

We gather close in twilight's glow,
Embracing all that we can know.
Through tears we water roots of hope,
In love's embrace, we learn to cope.

For life persists beyond the veil,
In every story yet to tell.
And though we ache, we shall not break,
In love's embrace, our souls awake.

So let the echoes softly chime,
In absence found, we break through time.
Together we rise, forever whole,
Through echoes of absence, we find our soul.

Breathing Life into Broken Dreams

In shadows deep where hope had fled,
The heart lies low, so bruised, so bled.
But gentle whispers float above,
A promise wrapped in boundless love.

Each breath we take, a gift divine,
Reviving dreams that once did shine.
With faith as light, our path will clear,
Restoring joy, dispelling fear.

The pieces scattered, fragile, torn,
In sacred hands, anew they're born.
Like phoenix rising from the ash,
We find the strength to make a dash.

Through trials faced and lessons learned,
In every heart, a fire burned.
Resilience blooms within the soul,
In broken dreams, we find our whole.

So let us lift our eyes up high,
To skies that stretch beyond the sigh.
For life once lost can breathe again,
In love's embrace, we'll rise, ascend.

The Alchemy of the Wandering Heart

A restless soul, on paths unknown,
Through valleys wide and mountains grown.
The heart seeks more, a quest unbound,
In every loss, a truth is found.

Each step we take, a dance divine,
With hands outstretched, we feel the sign.
For every tear that stains the cheek,
A lesson lies, a truth we seek.

In silence deep, where spirits roam,
We find the light that guides us home.
The journey teaches, wild and free,
Transforming pain to destiny.

With every heartbeat, wisdom grows,
Through wandering paths, forgiveness flows.
A sacred bond, the earth we tread,
In love's embrace, the heart is lead.

So wander forth, O brave and bold,
The tales of life are yet untold.
In each encounter, grace abounds,
The alchemy of love resounds.

Abundance from the Ashes

From ashes cold, a spark ignites,
In barren lands, a song delights.
With faith as fuel, the soul takes flight,
From darkest night, emerges light.

The seeds of hope in soil once gray,
Sprout vibrant blooms in bright array.
Through trials faced, we rise anew,
In every heart, the power grew.

A harvest rich, from sorrow's cry,
The spirit dances, reaching high.
In every setback, strength resides,
Through storms of life, our faith abides.

The tears we shed, like rain's sweet kiss,
Nurture the roots, transform the bliss.
In unity, our fears set free,
Abundance flows, eternally.

So from the ashes, let us rise,
With open hearts and fearless eyes.
Embrace the gifts that life bestows,
For through the pain, the light still glows.

Reawakening the Silent Soul

In quiet moments, peace we find,
A whisper soft, a voice unkind.
The soul, once hushed, begins to sing,
Awakening the joy within.

Through stillness deep, in nature's grace,
We seek the truth, we find our place.
With every breath, the spirit grows,
In quietude, the heart bestows.

A journey inward, vast and wide,
Where shadows lurk, yet light will bide.
With every tear, a tale unfolds,
In silence deep, the truth is told.

The world may roar, yet here we stand,
In whispered prayers, we feel God's hand.
For in the stillness, love will dwell,
Reawakening the soul's sweet shell.

So heed the call, O silent heart,
From gentle whispers, do not part.
In every pause, divinity's play,
Awakens life, shows us the way.

Rescued from the Depths of Dismay

In shadows deep, a whisper calls,
Through darkest nights, the spirit falls.
Yet hope ascends like morning light,
God's grace descends to end the night.

From depths of sorrow, hearts are freed,
Each tear a promise, each pain a seed.
With faith as anchor, souls arise,
In love's embrace, despair complies.

The weary traveler finds their way,
In silent prayers, the lost will stay.
In burdens shared, the heart is whole,
As mercy weaves, restoring soul.

Oft we stumble, oft we stray,
In grace's arms, we learn to pray.
A hand extended, a lifeline grand,
With every step, we understand.

Rescued from depths where shadows chase,
We rise anew in His embrace.
Through trials faced with courage bold,
Our faith endures, our spirits hold.

The Voices of the Abandoned

In alleys dark, where shadows creep,
The voices rise, the lost we keep.
Forgotten hearts, a silent plea,
In cracked and broken, eyes we see.

Yet still a light shines through the gloom,
A promise speaks from barren tombs.
For every tear that stains the ground,
God hears their cries, their souls unbound.

In whispers soft, they call for grace,
For love to fill this hollow space.
Among the wreckage, beauty grows,
In hands outstretched, compassion flows.

The weary walk this lonely mile,
Yet hope ignites within a smile.
For every heart that feels alone,
In faith, they rise, the seeds are sown.

No longer lost, they find their song,
Each note a truth where they belong.
In unity, their spirits soar,
For love has opened every door.

The Serpent and the Seraph

In garden lush, a tale unfolds,
Where serpent whispers, truth is sold.
Yet seraph stands with wings of light,
A guardian bold against the night.

With cunning words that tempt the heart,
The serpent weaves a subtle art.
But faith ignites like fire's glow,
The seraph's song rebukes the foe.

In every struggle, shadows loom,
Yet silver linings chase the gloom.
For battles fought with heaven's might,
The serpent quakes before the light.

In trials faced, we must decide,
To heed the voice, to fight or hide.
With courage found in love's embrace,
We choose the path, we seek His face.

So let the seraph lead us clear,
Through valleys steep, we cast our fear.
In unity, the truth shall reign,
The serpent's lies, we shall disdain.

Embraced by Eternal Solitude

In quietude, the soul takes flight,
Through realms of thought, in endless night.
Yet solitude, a tender balm,
In silence found, we find our calm.

The world may buzz with fickle sound,
But here within, true peace is found.
In whispered prayers, our hearts connect,
In solitude, we find respect.

In every heartbeat, echoes sway,
The Spirit moves in softest way.
In sacred hush, we learn to see,
The depths of love, eternity.

For every burden that we bear,
In whispered grace, we share our care.
As shadows fade, and dawn appears,
In solitude, we shed our fears.

Embraced by time, both vast and kind,
In solitude, true joy we find.
In every moment, grace unfolds,
In loving arms, our story holds.

Threads of Grace Woven Through Time

In the still light of dawn, hope unfurls,
With whispered dreams and sacred pearls.
Hands reaching forth in earnest prayer,
Threads of grace weave everywhere.

Each heart a tapestry of holy design,
Struggles and joys in love align.
Through trials faced and laughter shared,
A path of mercy, divinely prepared.

The rivers of faith run deep and wide,
Grace flows freely, a gentle tide.
In every moment, His presence shines,
Binding our souls with love's confines.

Across the ages, His promise stands,
Fingers entwined in divine hands.
Through shadows cast and light divine,
Threads of grace forever entwined.

The Burden of Forgotten Angels

In silent wings of night, they weep,
Forgotten souls in shadows deep.
A song unsung, a prayer unheard,
The burden borne without a word.

In corners dim where hope has fled,
Angels linger for the lost and dead.
Their whispers call from heaven's shore,
Awakening hearts to love once more.

Through veils of sorrow, their voices soar,
A light that beckons, forever implore.
In every tear, a promise stays,
The burden lightens through endless praise.

Yet in their plight, a light ignites,
Reminding us of truth's delights.
For every fallen, there's grace to find,
In the burden shared, our hearts aligned.

A Prayer for the Wayward Soul

Oh wanderer lost in the wild night,
Seek the warmth of love's pure light.
Through chaos and pain, find your way,
Turn your heart, do not delay.

In valleys low and mountains steep,
The Keeper of souls, His vow you keep.
Whispers of mercy, calm your fears,
A prayer offered, washed in tears.

Every misstep, a chance to rise,
With open arms and loving eyes.
He sees your struggle, He knows your name,
In every shadow, His love's the same.

So take a step, though weary and frail,
The road is paved with grace's trail.
In the echo of prayer, you shall find,
The wayward soul, forever entwined.

The Echo of Ancient Sorrows

Beneath the stars, the ancients sigh,
Their echoes linger, never die.
In every stone, a tale remains,
Of lost loves and forgotten pains.

Through fractured dreams and haunting nights,
The weight of history ignites.
Whispers of sorrow in the breeze,
A communion of spirits brings us to our knees.

In shadows cast by time's embrace,
We seek the truth, the hidden grace.
For every burden, a story tells,
Of heartache borne in quiet spells.

Yet in the twilight, hope appears,
Healing the wounds across the years.
For through the sorrow, a light shall break,
The echo of love, our hearts awake.

The Hidden Garden of Transcendence

In the stillness of the night,
Whispers of the divine are found.
Beneath the stars so bright,
Hearts awaken, souls unbound.

Petals fall like sacred tears,
Nurtured by heavenly light.
In this garden, cast your fears,
Find the path to eternal sight.

Fruits of wisdom gently grow,
In silence, love's embrace,
Where faith and nature flow,
Lost in grace's warm embrace.

Every breath, a prayer is spun,
In the breeze, the spirit sings.
In this haven, all is one,
Beyond the weight of worldly things.

Harvest peace and sow delight,
In the soil, grace does dwell.
In this hidden realm of light,
Transcendence, our miracle.

In Search of the Celestial Map

Stars above, a guiding flame,
Chart my path through night's deep grace.
In the dark, I call Your name,
Illuminate my soul's embrace.

Wanderlust of heart and mind,
Through the cosmos, I will roam.
In Your love, I seek and find,
Each step leading me back home.

Every soul a shining star,
Lost but found in sacred song.
In Your light, I'll travel far,
True to You, I will belong.

Mysteries unfold each night,
Constellations brightly lie.
In their dance, I seek Your light,
In this vast and wondrous sky.

So grant me, Lord, a compass true,
To navigate this sacred quest.
In the map of love, renew,
Found in faith, forever blessed.

The Journey Back to Bethlehem

With every step, a prayer I trace,
To the cradle where love once lay.
Guided by the stars' soft grace,
In my heart, a light will play.

Dusty roads and travelers near,
Seek the birthplace, pure and bright.
In the stillness, draw me near,
Where hope shines in the night.

Echoes of angels' sweet refrain,
Fill the air with joy untold.
Through the trials, through the pain,
In Your warmth, my heart turns bold.

Melodies of prayer arise,
In the stillness, faith is sown.
With a heart that softly cries,
I journey back, no more alone.

In this sacred, humble place,
Love's embrace will ever stay.
As I seek the holy face,
Bethlehem, lead me to the way.

Mysteries of the Silent Sanctuary

In the quiet of the morn,
Where the spirit seeks repose,
Within these walls, a heart reborn,
In silence, every secret grows.

Candles flicker with a glow,
Spilling warmth on hallowed ground.
In each shadow, truth will flow,
A peace within, profound.

Here the whispers softly call,
Echoes of the past remain.
In this space, we stand in awe,
In the stillness, love's refrain.

Veils of mystery do unfold,
In the presence of the divine.
Through each story, love is told,
In the heart, a sacred sign.

So let us dwell in quiet grace,
In this sanctuary, find our rest.
With every breath, we seek Your face,
In Your arms, forever blessed.

A Pilgrim's Silent Tear

In the stillness of the night,
A pilgrim walks alone,
With every step, a whisper,
His heart, a heavy stone.

He seeks the grace of heaven,
A light to guide his way,
But shadows cling around him,
As dawn begins to sway.

Each tear a prayer unspoken,
Each sigh a sacred plea,
In the silence of his journey,
He longs to be set free.

Through valleys deep and dark,
His faith begins to strain,
Yet still he holds the lantern,
To spark the hope in pain.

At last, he finds the river,
That flows with love and grace,
His silent tear now whispers,
"Here, I have found my place."

The Light That Once Guided

Once a beacon in the night,
The light that held my soul,
Now flickers in the distance,
A distant, fading goal.

Through storms of doubt and worry,
I wander lost, alone,
Yearning for the warmth of comfort,
To guide me back home.

Yet echoes of your promise,
Still linger in the air,
A reminder of the grace,
That once was always there.

I search for truth in silence,
Where shadows dare to creep,
And even in the darkness,
I find the strength to weep.

For though the path is winding,
And the night is long and deep,
I carry hope within me,
A light I vow to keep.

Remnants of the Silent Prayer

In the quiet of the morning,
A heart begins to plead,
For remnants of the solace,
That nourished every need.

Each word, a gentle echo,
Of whispers lost in time,
I seek the path to grace,
In rhythm and in rhyme.

Amidst the wreckage of my doubts,
I gather thoughts unsaid,
A tapestry of wishes,
Where faith and hope are wed.

Through hours trapped in stillness,
I find the strength to stand,
And every silent prayer,
Rises like grains of sand.

With every breath, I cherish,
The fragments of my cries,
In the depths of my spirit,
A dawn begins to rise.

Where the Soul Goes Astray

In valleys vast and lonely,
The soul begins to roam,
Seeking love, a spark of light,
To guide it safely home.

But wandering brings confusion,
And shadows veil the way,
A heart weighed down with questions,
In places lost and gray.

Yet in the depths of silence,
The spirit starts to mend,
In searching for the beauty,
To find the heart's true friend.

With every step a lesson,
Through trials, pain, and tears,
I learn to trust the journey,
To conquer all my fears.

For even when I falter,
And feel the world's dismay,
My soul will rise as morning,
To greet a brand new day.

The Return of the Wayward Spirit

In the shadows, the spirit roams,
Searching for a place called home.
With heavy heart, it seeks the light,
A whispered prayer to end the night.

Guided by the stars above,
The warmth of grace, the pulse of love.
Each step taken draws it near,
To the embrace that dries each tear.

In the stillness, a voice is found,
A sacred echo, soft and sound.
Crimson skies and open seas,
The call of faith, the gentle breeze.

With open arms, the heavens sing,
Of peace restored and hope in spring.
The wayward spirit finds its peace,
In the arms of love, its sweet release.

Now reunited, the soul takes flight,
Dancing in the warm, golden light.
A voyage ends, but yet begins,
In sacred trust, redemption wins.

Echoes Beneath the Altar

In hushed tones, the whispers rise,
Voices woven through the skies.
Beneath the altar, secrets lay,
The heart of sorrow, the soul's true way.

Candle flames flicker, shadows play,
Each flicker tells what words can't say.
In sacred space, burdens unbound,
Lay the hopes that once were drowned.

Hearts unyielding, bowed in prayer,
Offering dreams laid bare in despair.
The echoes of faith beckon near,
A promise made, a path made clear.

Through the silence, a hymn resounds,
In the marrow where love abounds.
For in the depths, redemption's key,
Unlocks the chains, sets the spirit free.

With every prayer, a seed is sown,
In hallowed ground, the light has grown.
Beneath the altar, hope ignites,
Each echo a beacon in darkest nights.

The Journey Toward Redemption

Across the valleys, through trials and tears,
The journey unfolds, vanquishing fears.
With every step, the heart grows strong,
Guided by faith, where souls belong.

Mountains may rise, and rivers may roar,
Yet the spirit knows what lies in store.
For shadows fade beneath the sun,
In the light, all battles are won.

Through tangled paths and winding roads,
Wisdom blossoms, truth erodes.
Each stumble teaches, each fall refines,
In the garden of grace, the heart aligns.

As dawn breaks forth, the past laid bare,
Forgiveness whispers in the air.
With open hands, the soul ascends,
In love's embrace, the journey mends.

The road may twist, yet steadfast we go,
In search of mercy, our spirits flow.
With every heartbeat, the promise sings,
Redemption unfolds on angel's wings.

Unveiling Hidden Blessings

In the quiet corners of the night,
Hidden blessings come to light.
In the stillness, grace abounds,
Miracles whispered in sacred sounds.

Through trials faced and burdens borne,
In life's tempests, new strengths are worn.
With gratitude, we count each gift,
In every struggle, our souls uplift.

The gentle rain that quenches the ground,
A tender touch, love all around.
In the smallest moments, truth reveals,
Life's tapestry, the heart it heals.

With open hearts, we learn to see,
The beauty woven in life's decree.
For every shadow serves a role,
In unveiling blessings, we find our soul.

As dawn breaks forth and dreams take flight,
We celebrate the love of light.
In each heartbeat, forever confess,
Life's hidden blessings are nothing less.

The Resurrection of Sacred Dreams

In darkness deep, where hope had fled,
The whisper of faith gently spread.
From ashes rise, the spirit gleams,
Awakening the sacred dreams.

In humble hearts the promise shines,
As love ignites the fractured lines.
With every prayer, a seed takes root,
In time, this truth will bear sweet fruit.

Through trials faced and burdens born,
The soul reborn, a brand new dawn.
With open arms, let welcome be,
Anointed by divinity.

In unity, we lift our gaze,
To find the light in all our days.
The path ahead, lit by the grace,
Of sacred dreams we all embrace.

So let us sing in harmony,
Of resurrection's symphony.
Together bound, we shall fulfill,
The sacred dreams that love instills.

Echoes of the Chosen Path

With every step on sacred ground,
The echoes of the past resound.
In faith we walk, through trials bold,
Adorned with love, our story told.

A winding road, the chosen way,
Where night gives birth to brightening day.
In every heart, the journey's flame,
Illuminates the Savior's name.

Through winding paths and peaceful glades,
The guidance of the Spirit wades.
Each moment cherished, each lesson learned,
In trust, the sacred fire burned.

Though shadows fall and storms may come,
In prayer, we find our hearts at home.
Together bound by sacred light,
With hope, we journey through the night.

Let every soul find strength and peace,
In love's embrace, our doubts release.
We'll walk the path the wise have trod,
In every step, we feel our God.

A Light Among the Shadows

In shadows cast, a beacon glows,
A light that through the darkness flows.
With every tear, we find our grace,
In love's embrace, we find our place.

Through trials faced, the heart grows strong,
In unity, we sing our song.
Guided by hope, we rise anew,
And let the light within us shine through.

With every doubt, our faith renews,
The dawn of day brings brighter hues.
In every soul, a spark resides,
With love's pure flame, our spirit guides.

We walk with grace, we walk with might,
Our steps aligned with the sacred light.
In every shadow, love will bloom,
Dispelling fear, dispelling gloom.

Together bound in sacred trust,
In faith we find what's true and just.
With hearts ablaze, we face the night,
For we are called to be the light.

The Forgotten Heart's Lament

In silence deep, the heart does weep,
For dreams of old, now lost in sleep.
In shadows cast, we seek the spark,
To mend the wounds that left their mark.

Once full of light, now dimmed by pain,
The echoes haunt like falling rain.
A whispered prayer, a longing sigh,
Awakens hope that will not die.

In every tear, a story dwells,
Of love once shared, of sacredels.
With gentle hands, we tend the soul,
To heal the heart and make it whole.

Through valleys low and mountains high,
Each step we take, our spirits fly.
For in the lament, there's grace to find,
A call to seek and be defined.

So let us rise on wings of prayer,
To find the peace that's always there.
In unity, we'll mend our hearts,
For love's true song will never part.

In the Whispering Shadow

In the hush of twilight's fold,
Whispers of grace begin to unfold.
Hearts attuned to the quiet night,
Seek the path to the hidden light.

Tested souls find solace here,
In shadows cast, they draw near.
With each breath, a prayer ascends,
In the stillness, mercy mends.

Heaven's echoes surround the meek,
In their silence, soft voices speak.
Guiding hands extend from above,
Through the dark, we feel their love.

Fear not the shadows that loom wide,
For in them, faith becomes our guide.
Each step forward, we walk as one,
In the whispering, grace is spun.

When dawn breaks over the land,
We rise anew, in His hand.
Through every whisper, every prayer,
We find our strength, we find our care.

Echoes of the Absent Heart

In the stillness, echoes call,
Hearts remember through it all.
Longing lingers in the air,
For the lost, a silent prayer.

Wanderers drift without a guide,
In shadows where their hopes reside.
Yet, grace flows like a gentle stream,
Awakens souls from a faded dream.

Though absent, love does not decay,
Faith's embrace shows the way.
Through trials faced and tears we shed,
In memories, our hearts are fed.

Light the candles of the night,
Let their glow be the sign of right.
In the silence, souls unite,
Rekindled hope brings forth the light.

Their voices rise, a chorus sweet,
In distant lands, our hearts still meet.
Echoes linger, never depart,
In every silence, love imparts.

The Wayward Pilgrim

Upon the road, a pilgrim treads,
Through valleys deep and riverbeds.
With each step, they seek the truth,
A journey worn by ancient youth.

Though paths diverge in shades unknown,
In every heart, a seed is sown.
Courage rises with morning's breath,
In trials faced, we conquer death.

Whispers guide through darkened woods,
Where faith endures, and hope intrudes.
With weary feet, but eyes ablaze,
The wayward find a holy gaze.

From distant shores to mountains high,
Every prayer is a whispered sigh.
The stars above, their compass bright,
Lead us forth towards the light.

When burdens weigh and spirits tire,
Lift our hearts, our souls inspire.
On this path, though fraught with strife,
The wayward pilgrim finds their life.

Souls Adrift in Sacred Silence

In sacred silence, lost souls drift,
Yearning hearts seek a precious gift.
Amidst the noise, they cry to be,
Anchored deep in the mystery.

Each moment still, their spirits rise,
Beneath the vast and watchful skies.
With boundless love, their hopes align,
In sacred space, where hearts entwine.

Through trembling hands, they reach for peace,
In silent prayers, their sorrows cease.
In patience, guidance softly flows,
As deeper wisdom gently grows.

Though adrift in life's great sea,
Their souls find strength in unity.
In trials faced, they learn to stand,
Together bound by love so grand.

In every pause, the spirit speaks,
Through quiet hearts, the truth it seeks.
Adrift no more, in grace we dwell,
In sacred silence, all is well.

The Sanctuary of Unseen Signs

In whispers dwells the sacred light,
Where shadows weave the threads of night.
Each breath a prayer, each heartbeat calls,
To the hidden grace that gently falls.

With eyes that seek the signs concealed,
In nature's hymn, the truth revealed.
The rustling leaves, the flowing stream,
In every moment, a silent dream.

Beneath the stars, our hearts entwined,
In solitude, the spirit finds.
The echoes of the past resound,
In the sanctuary, peace is found.

Awake, oh soul, to sacred space,
Where love and hope embrace each grace.
The unseen signs, a guiding hand,
In faith, united, we shall stand.

Fear not the silence, let it speak,
In tender trust, we gently seek.
Each step a testament of the heart,
In the unseen, we play our part.

Finding Grace Amongst the Ruins

Amidst the crumbling stones and dust,
Where dreams once thrived in fervent trust.
A whisper of hope, a flicker of grace,
In the ruins, we find our place.

The shadows linger, but light breaks through,
In every trial, our spirits renew.
Where sorrow sleeps in silent gloom,
A seed of joy begins to bloom.

With hands outstretched, we seek the dawn,
In the fragile spaces, we're reborn.
The past may weep, but futures gleam,
In the ashes, we foster dreams.

Let every stone tell a story grand,
Of love lost, and bonds that stand.
Through brokenness, our souls arise,
Finding grace 'neath sorrowed skies.

Together we stand, united strong,
In the ruins, we sing our song.
With faith restored, we lift our eyes,
Finding hope where the heart cries.

The Lost Pages of the Soul

In forgotten corners of the mind,
Lie pages lost, the heart may find.
Whispers of stories yet untold,
In the silence, treasures unfold.

Each line inscribed with love and pain,
The dance of joy, the pulse of rain.
Ink of memories, fading light,
In shadows cast, we seek the bright.

The book of life, with tears and smiles,
In every chapter, we walk the miles.
From darkened depths, to peaks that soar,
The lost pages beckon us to explore.

With every turn, we heal the heart,
In life's vast tome, we play our part.
To the ink of dreams, we raise a toast,
In the lost pages, we find our ghost.

Awakened now, with courage bold,
To share our tales, let them unfold.
In unity, we turn each page,
The lost pages of the soul, our stage.

The Pilgrim's Quiet Return

Through valleys deep and mountains high,
The pilgrim walks, beneath the sky.
In weary steps, the heart compresses,
To find the peace that life obsesses.

With every breath, a story spun,
In every shadow, the light begun.
The trials faced, the lessons learned,
In quiet moments, the spirit turned.

Homeward bound with grace anew,
The pilgrim's path, in skies so blue.
With open arms, a welcome song,
In every fiber, we all belong.

The echoes of the journey sway,
With every dawn, a brand new way.
Through laughter shared and burdens borne,
In every heart, a bond is sworn.

So let the past, in peace collide,
As dreams walk forth, and love abides.
The pilgrim's quiet return is here,
Embraced by grace, dispelling fear.

Secrets of the Celestial Map

In the night sky, stars whisper low,
Guiding our hearts where waters flow.
Each twinkle a promise, a glimmering light,
Leading us home through the veil of night.

Planets align, in their heavenly dance,
Their orbits a testament, a sacred chance.
We seek their wisdom, in shadows they dwell,
Unraveling secrets, we strive to tell.

Constellations form stories, etched in the dark,
A divine cartography, igniting the spark.
With faith as our compass, our souls take flight,
Navigating dreams through the infinite night.

Awakened by dawn, the stars fade away,
Yet their echoes linger, a soft chorus play.
For in every heartbeat, lies a sacred map,
To the mysteries woven in the heavenly lap.

So look to the sky, where the answers reside,
The secrets of life in the starlight abide.
In the vastness above, our spirits ascend,
To grasp the divine hand, as we journey and mend.

The Silent Return of Faith

Amidst the chaos, a stillness we find,
Whispers of grace in the echoes of time.
Each prayer a flower, blooming anew,
A testament of love, in the heart's gentle hue.

When shadows encroach, and doubts fill the air,
A flicker of hope, a moment to share.
In silence, we gather, in reverence stand,
Rekindling the light, with a steady hand.

The journey unfolds, with valleys and peaks,
In the language of faith, it's solace that speaks.
Though storms may rage, and tempests may roar,
In the silence of trust, we're anchored once more.

Steps taken in faith are the path to behold,
In the warmth of belief, our stories unfold.
As the sun rises high, our spirits awake,
In the dawn of true faith, we find what we seek.

So listen for whispers, in moments of grace,
The silent return, in this holy space.
For in quiet submission, we find our way home,
In the heart of the Divine, is where we are known.

Beneath the Weight of Lost Tomorrows

Heavy the heart, with burdens we bear,
Dreams left unspoken, suspended in air.
But in the stillness, grace starts to flow,
Revealing the path that we yearn to know.

Every tear fallen, a pearl of the soul,
Creating a necklace, a story made whole.
In the depths of despair, a seed takes its root,
For love's gentle touch is the sweetest pursuit.

As shadows may linger, the dawn brings release,
A promise of healing, a whisper of peace.
From the ashes of sorrow, we rise with the sun,
Transforming our trials, for the battle's not won.

In moments of doubt, let faith be your guide,
With each step of courage, you're never denied.
Beneath the weight of what once was lost,
New tomorrows await, no matter the cost.

So gather the fragments, the light from the past,
In the tapestry woven, we find peace at last.
For every lost tomorrow births tomorrow anew,
A testament of strength, in all that we do.

A Testament in Shadows

In the quiet of night, where shadows converge,
A testament whispers, our spirits emerge.
In the dance of the dark, there's wonder and grace,
For even in silence, we find our own place.

Every heartbeat echoes, a song from within,
In the depths of the dark, our journey begins.
With courage ignited, we rise from the gloom,
A testament forged in the heart's sacred room.

As the moonlight cascades, casting hope on the land,
In the arms of the night, we take a firm stand.
For shadows may linger, but light will abide,
A testament of faith, our spirits as guide.

Beyond the horizon, dawn breaks at last,
Embracing the lessons that shadows have cast.
In every dark corner, a seed has been sown,
A testament in shadows, our legacy grown.

So fear not the night, nor the depths of despair,
For shadows are fleeting, and light's always there.
In the tapestry woven, our stories unite,
A testament of love, born from the night.

The Celestial Glimmers in the Dark

In shadows deep, a light will glow,
A gentle whisper, soft and low.
Guiding hearts through trials unseen,
In the night, the stars convene.

A promise held in each bright spark,
Faith ignites, ignites the dark.
Through the veil of time and space,
Hope transcends, a sweet embrace.

In every tear, a lesson shines,
Grace unfolds in sacred signs.
The heavens sing, their voices blend,
To remind us love is without end.

Beneath the weight of fleeting days,
A stronger light begins to blaze.
Like candles held in trembling hands,
Our spirits soar, as faith expands.

When all seems lost and shadows loom,
The celestial glimmers break the gloom.
In our hearts, an eternal flame,
In the night, we call His name.

The Doorway to Hidden Blessings

Knock upon the door of grace,
With humble heart and seeking face.
Inside, a wealth of love awaits,
Unseen wonders, open gates.

Each step we take, the path unfolds,
In every story, truth beholds.
Wisdom whispers from the past,
In silence, blessings come at last.

The weary traveler finds a seat,
Where quiet souls and kind hearts meet.
The warmth of hope, a sacred bond,
In the depths, we all respond.

If joy eludes, come taste and see,
A banquet laid, God's work is free.
The doorway wide, with arms held fast,
In His embrace, we find our cast.

Each blessing hidden, yet so near,
In faith's embrace, we conquer fear.
With open hearts, we share the light,
Guided by love, our spirits' flight.

A Journey Homeward in Silence

In quietude, the soul takes flight,
Through valleys deep, to mountain height.
With every breath, the world awakes,
In stillness, love's vibration shakes.

Paths may wane, and shadows fall,
Yet whispers guide through nature's call.
The heart knows well where to abide,
In humble grace, we do confide.

Each gentle step sheds worldly care,
In solitude, we learn to bear.
The journey home, though fraught with pain,
In silence, truth and peace remain.

The light within ignites the way,
Leading souls to brighter day.
With faith as map, and hope as key,
A journey homeward, wild and free.

As stars align, and spirits soar,
In this silence, we seek more.
The quest for love, forever new,
A journey home, a bond so true.

Where the Spirit Once Roamed

In ancient woods where whispers dwell,
The spirit's voice, a timeless bell.
Each rustling leaf, a tale retold,
Of sacred truths, both brave and bold.

The river flows with memories deep,
Where laughter danced and shadows creep.
In every stone, a life once lived,
A reminder of the love we give.

Beneath the arch of sky so vast,
The footprints linger; echoes cast.
In sacred sites, connection reigns,
Where spirit wanders, love remains.

With every dawn, a chance to see,
The beauty born from all that be.
A pilgrimage through sacred space,
In every heart, we find our place.

Where the spirit once roamed, we continue,
With open hearts, inspired anew.
In nature's arms, we find our peace,
In loving echoes, sweet release.

The Hymn of the Forgotten Pilgrimage

In silence we tread, the road long and wide,
Each step a prayer, in faith we abide.
Whispers of angels, guiding our will,
Hope in our hearts, a vision to fulfill.

Upon distant shores, our dreams are a flame,
With tears of the past, we'll rise once again.
Through shadows and doubt, to honor the quest,
The spirit entwined, in heavenly rest.

Mountains of glory, we climb to the light,
With burdens we carry, we seek what is right.
The song of the dawn breaks chains we have worn,
In unity's voice, our souls will be reborn.

Each valley we cross, though weary and worn,
Reminds us of grace, in the trials we've borne.
Beneath the arching sky, our hearts will ignite,
In pilgrimage's glow, embracing the night.

So let us rejoice, as the stars now appear,
For even in distance, the love draws us near.
Together we wander, forever in praise,
The hymn of the journey, through life's winding maze.

Beneath the Stars of Grace

In the hush of the night, the heavens unfold,
Stories of mercy, and love's embrace told.
Beneath the vast canopy, dreams softly soar,
Guided by starlight, we seek and explore.

The moon whispers secrets, so tender and bright,
Bathing the world in its silvery light.
Each twinkle above, a divine assurance,
Reminds us to trust in our hearts' purest currents.

Gathered as pilgrims, we share in the glow,
Awash in the warmth, through valleys we flow.
With hands clasped in faith, our spirits entwined,
We rise in the darkness, in peace we will find.

Every moment a gift, in this sacred space,
Finding our strength, beneath stars of grace.
So let us be vessels of love and of light,
Embracing the journey, forever in sight.

With every dawn breaking, our hearts will proclaim,
The love that unites us, all honor the same.
Together we rise, as the world holds its breath,
Beneath the stars shining, in life after death.

Finding the Path in Darkness

When shadows surround and hope starts to fade,
The heart whispers softly; do not be afraid.
In silence we listen, the truth crystal clear,
A path will emerge, if we hold what is dear.

The night may be long, but the dawn will arise,
Illuminating dreams, and our steadfast ties.
With lanterns of faith, we walk hand in hand,
Through valleys of sorrow, together we stand.

With every step forward, the burdens grow light,
In the arms of our brotherhood, we spark the bright.
For every dark moment is a lesson concealed,
A gift from the heavens, our fate is revealed.

In the darkest of hours, a beacon will glow,
Guiding our spirits, wherever we go.
Determined and brave, our hearts resonate,
Finding the path, for we shall not wait.

So take heart, dear friend, in the trials we face,
For light will return, and we'll bask in its grace.
Through darkness we travel, let love be our guide,
For together we flourish, with faith at our side.

Through the Eyes of the Lost

In moments of darkness, our vision might blur,
Yet in our confusion, love will confer.
Through eyes that are weary, we search for the light,
Hoping to find grace within the longest night.

The weight of our struggles may bend us in pain,
But strength lies in stories, no trial in vain.
For each soul we meet, a mirror we see,
Reflecting our journeys, how we long to be free.

With hearts that are open, we share and we learn,
In the fellowship found, our passions will burn.
Through the eyes of the lost, we find our way home,
Unearthing the truths in this vast world we roam.

For every misstep is a path to embrace,
Emerging from shadows into love's warm embrace.
Together we wander, as seekers of grace,
Through the eyes of the lost, the divine we will trace.

So when you feel lost, look around and find,
The beauty of kindness, an unbreakable bind.
In fellowship gathered, we rise from the frost,
Finding our purpose as we roam with the lost.

The Unending Quest for Light

In shadows deep, we seek the dawn,
A flicker guides where faith is drawn.
With hearts ablaze, we rise and soar,
To find the light forevermore.

Through valleys low and mountains high,
The whispered prayers ascend the sky.
With every step, a hope ignites,
In pursuit of sacred, warming lights.

The path is rough, yet beauty shines,
In every struggle, love entwines.
The starry night, a canvas wide,
Our souls shall wander, hand in hand, side by side.

With every tear, a lesson learned,
In darkest nights, our spirits turned.
A glowing ember within our core,
Awakens strength and yearns for more.

Together we'll ignite the flame,
In unity we'll share His name.
The unending quest shall never cease,
In light's embrace, we find our peace.

Reading the Signs of Dusk

As evening falls, the shadows play,
In silence whispers words to say.
The horizon glows with hues divine,
Each fading sunbeams softly shine.

The stars emerge, the moon awakes,
In twilight's grasp, the spirit breaks.
With every sigh, a truth concealed,
The mysteries of dusk revealed.

Nature calls in gentle tones,
Her secret paths, the heart atones.
Each rustling leaf, a sacred text,
In reverence, we ponder next.

In quiet moments, wisdom flows,
As shadows deepen, insight grows.
With humbled hearts, we seek to find,
The signs of dusk, the voice of mind.

Embrace the dark as light shall flee,
For in these hours, we come to see.
The night reveals both peace and strife,
In binding grace, we glean our life.

The Path We Have Not Tread

With every step, the journey calls,
The unmarked way where silence falls.
A path unknown, yet known by heart,
Each choice we make can set apart.

The morning mist conceals our way,
Yet faith shall guide us, come what may.
Through doubts and fears, we shall advance,
In every trial, a chance to dance.

Though thorns may prickle, wildflowers bloom,
Each moment's struggle yields room for room.
The sacred trust fuels our reward,
In the journey, we embrace the Lord.

In realms unseen, His light shall gleam,
A brighter path than what we dream.
With every breath, we pave the track,
In grace we walk, we shan't look back.

Through uncharted lands, we rise anew,
For hope shall guide as we pursue.
Our hearts entwined, as one we tread,
On the path of faith, not fear or dread.

Requiem for the Heart's Soliloquy

In silence deep, the heart does speak,
A melody of all we seek.
The echoes of a soul laid bare,
In whispered tones, a sacred prayer.

For every tear, a lesson finds,
A requiem that shapes our minds.
With joy and sorrow intertwined,
The dance of faith shall not unwind.

In solitude, reflections glow,
A journey inward, deep and slow.
Each heartbeat yields a story spun,
In shadows bright, the light begun.

With open hearts, we gather close,
To share the burdens, fears, and hopes.
In solemn grace, we weave our song,
A testament that we belong.

As life unfolds, we rise and fall,
In harmony, we heed the call.
This requiem, a sacred rite,
Unveiling truth, embracing light.

Beneath the Shattered Halo

In shadows thick, the angels weep,
Their silver wings, a promise steep.
The echoes of a song long sung,
Now lost in silence, old and young.

Yet hope ignites in faintest spark,
A flicker bright within the dark.
From broken dreams, new paths emerge,
A whispered prayer, a silent urge.

The echoes of the past still call,
In whispered chants, we stand or fall.
With every tear, a lesson learned,
In ashes of the faith we've burned.

Beneath the halo, shattered, worn,
We seek the light, though hope is torn.
In every heart, a seed is sown,
To rise again, to find a home.

For every soul that's lost its way,
Beneath the shards, a new doorway.
In faith reborn, we rise anew,
Beneath the sky, still vast and blue.

The Forgotten Covenant

In ancient tomes, the whispers dwell,
Of pacts once bold, of hope's sweet swell.
Where promises like starlight shone,
Now shadows cloak the seeds we've sown.

The altar lies in dust and gloom,
Where fervent prayers conceit to bloom.
Forgotten vows in silence fade,
Yet in their wake, new dreams are made.

Between the lines of sacred text,
A truth emerges, forth perplexed.
Revived in hearts that dare to seek,
In brokenness, the strong can speak.

We gather strength from stories lost,
To count the cost, we bear the frost.
In every heart, a fire burns,
For every choice, a lesson learns.

So let us forge a new decree,
Embrace the past, and set it free.
For in the dust of ages past,
A covenant that holds steadfast.

Fragments of Faith in Hallowed Ground

Among the stones, where shadows play,
In hallowed ground, we kneel and pray.
Each fragment speaks of battles won,
A journey marked, a race begun.

The echoes linger, soft yet clear,
In every sigh, a whispered cheer.
For every heart that seeks the light,
In darkest hours, a spark ignites.

Through trials faced, in valleys deep,
We weave our hopes, our dreams we keep.
In fragments found, a mosaic made,
Of faith renewed, unafraid.

Each stone a story, rich and vast,
Of joyful days and sorrows past.
For in the cracks, where shadows blend,
We find the balm that spirits mend.

As moonlight casts its silver glow,
The seeds of faith in silence grow.
With hearts entwined, we walk the line,
In hallowed spaces, souls align.

Wandering Through Divine Despair

In the desert, where hope seems lost,
I wander wide, exploring the cost.
Each grain of sand a whispered prayer,
In the silence, I seek to dare.

The heavens weep with every sigh,
As clouds drift slow, like dreams that fly.
In shadows cast by doubt and fear,
I hear the echoes of love draw near.

Yet in the distance, a beacon glows,
With every step, my spirit grows.
Though paths are rough and burdens weigh,
In solitude, I find my way.

For every tear that stains the ground,
A promise waits, in grace profound.
Through trials tough, I find my voice,
In sorrow's depth, I still rejoice.

So on I roam, with faith as guide,
Through seasons dark, with God beside.
In wandering forth, my spirit soars,
In divine despair, I seek the shores.

Redemption in the Ruins of History

Amidst the stones where shadows dwell,
Time whispers tales that Heaven can tell.
In broken places, hope takes its stand,
Hands of the faithful weave love through the land.

Grace springs forth from the ashes of grief,
In every sorrow, there's a hidden belief.
Hearts lifted high, through the veil of despair,
Find solace in faith, for He is aware.

From the depth of darkness, light will arise,
A promise of mercy in the endless skies.
With each step we take on this sacred ground,
The echoes of redemption in His love are found.

Ashes may settle, but seeds gently sown,
In the soil of the lost, our spirits have grown.
Through trials endured, the spirit is free,
In the ruins of history, we find our decree.

Bound by His mercy, we rise from the dust,
With courage and faith, in Him we trust.
Amid the decay, His promise is true,
Redemption awaits; for me and for you.

The Grace of the Abandoned

In the quiet corners where shadows reside,
The grace of the abandoned cannot hide.
Whispers of love linger still in the air,
Embracing the lonely with tender care.

While life may forsake, the spirit remains,
In every lost heart, a heartbeat still reigns.
Hands once forgotten now reach for the light,
The grace of the abandoned shines ever bright.

From hollowed chambers to the streets of despair,
Each soul bears the image of love found in prayer.
In the world's harsh judgement, one heart shall behold,
The warmth of redemption, a story retold.

Through the tears of the broken, new strength will appear,

In the silence of night, He draws ever near.
With every soft sigh, let hope bloom like spring,
The grace of the abandoned, to life will bring.

Together we rise from shadows long cast,
For His love endures through the trials we've passed.
In the arms of the weary, we'll learn to believe,
That grace shines the brightest when we're left to grieve.

Fragments of Sacred Longing

In the tapestry woven with threads of the soul,
Each fragment of longing finds purpose and whole.
Hearts ache with whispers of dreams left unsaid,
In silence, we gather what love gently bled.

Through valleys of yearning, we wander alone,
Yet fragments of sacred remind us we're known.
A flicker of light shines through desolate skies,
In the depths of our being, His promise replies.

Each sorrow a seed, in darkness it's sown,
In gardens of hope, our spirits have grown.
While fate may divide us, love's thread will entwine,
Fragments of sacred, forever divine.

With hearts wide open, we seek and we find,
The essence of grace in the ties that bind.
In the stillness, His presence softly calls,
Each fragment united, together we stand tall.

From the depths of our longing, new dreams will arise,
In the echoes of faith, our spirits will rise.
Together we'll gather the pieces that wait,
Fragments of sacred, renewed by His fate.

The Light that Guides the Weary

In the shadowy paths where hope starts to fade,
The light that guides weary hearts must be made.
Through trials and tempest, He walks by our side,
In every dark moment, He'll be our guide.

When burdens weigh heavy and courage is lost,
The path that we wander is shaped by the cost.
Yet gently He beckons, 'fear not, my friend,'
For light shines through darkness and love has no end.

In whispers of kindness, His promise resounds,
Through valleys of shadows, His grace knows no bounds.

Trust in the journey, though fraught with despair,
For the light that guides weary will always be there.

Hope flickers softly like stars in the night,
Each moment a chance to embrace His light.
In the arms of His mercy, let go of our fight,
For weary souls find peace wrapped in His sight.

As dawn greets the world, let our spirits rejoice,
In the glow of His presence, we find our true voice.
Through trials endured, let our hearts sing and soar,
For the light that guides the weary forevermore.

Treading the Path of Forgotten Wisdom

In shadows deep, the ancients dwell,
Their whispers echo, a mystic spell.
Through hallowed ground, the seekers tread,
Finding solace where the lost are fed.

Beneath the stars, the stories bloom,
Each star a soul, escaping gloom.
A sacred fire ignites the night,
Illuminating the path of right.

With every step, the heart finds grace,
In quiet corners, a sacred place.
The wisdom of ages, softly calls,
In nature's embrace, the spirit enthralls.

Echoes of truth in the wind do sigh,
Where once the faithful dared to fly.
Treading lightly on the earth so blessed,
With reverence found, our souls find rest.

So walk with peace, let your heart unfold,
In ancient dreams, the stories told.
Within the silence, the answers lie,
Treading the path, where spirits fly.

The Crossroads of Renewal

At dawn's first light, new paths arise,
With whispered hopes beneath the skies.
The heart beats strong at the turn of fate,
In stillness found, we contemplate.

Each choice a step, each breath a prayer,
In the sacred winds, we lay our care.
Renewal flows like a gentle stream,
Awakening souls to a timeless dream.

Beneath the burden, the spirit soars,
Breaking the chains, opening doors.
In every trial, we find the light,
The crossroads guide us, day turns to night.

Together we stand, hand in hand,
Facing the horizon, a promised land.
With every moment, a grace bestowed,
In love's embrace, the heart's abode.

So let us walk, in joy and peace,
At the crossroads where our fears cease.
Where souls unite, and voices blend,
In renewal's grace, we find our end.

Between the Veils of Time

Time weaves a tapestry, rich and bold,
Stories of life, silently told.
Each thread intertwined, past with the now,
In the sacred dance, we learn to bow.

Between the whispers, a truth resides,
In every heartbeat, the spirit guides.
Moments of stillness where the world fades,
Between the veils, the light cascades.

In the echoing silence, wisdom speaks,
Through trials and tears, the heart seeks.
A journey of ages within our soul,
Breaking the chains, we become whole.

So gather the dreams, let them take flight,
In timeless embrace, we find the light.
Between the veils, our spirits align,
In the essence of love, we forever shine.

With reverence held for the past we cherish,
In the light of the now, we shall not perish.
Time's sacred dance, a circle divine,
Between the veils, our souls entwine.

The Altar Where They Once Knelt

In solemn grace, the altar stands,
Where prayers were whispered, by faithful hands.
Upon the stones, the echoes we find,
Of hearts once joined, in spirit aligned.

Candle flames flicker, casting light,
Guiding the lost through the depths of night.
With every tear, a story flows,
In sacred spaces, love forever glows.

The air is thick with reverent sighs,
As time surrenders, beneath the skies.
In silent moments, the past ignites,
At the altar, our hope reunites.

So come and kneel, in the quiet embrace,
Find solace here, in this cherished place.
Where souls once gathered in unity's glow,
The altar whispers what we need to know.

With every breath, we honor the pain,
In love's remembrance, lose not, but gain.
At this sacred site, let the heart swell,
In the stories shared, at the altar they knelt.

The Cradle of Lost Intentions

In shadows where whispers dwell,
Dreams have paused, silence fell.
Hearts once bold, now in despair,
Seek refuge in breath of prayer.

Yet, hope flickers in the dark,
A faint glow, a cherished spark.
God's embrace, a gentle guide,
Through storms, we will abide.

Remember the promises made,
Before the cares of life invade.
For every tear that trials send,
A seed of grace will transcend.

In the cradle of lost dreams,
Faith revives, or so it seems.
Hearts, though weary, still will rise,
To claim anew the endless skies.

Let each intention find its way,
Through paths of love, come what may.
In surrender, we learn to trust,
And see the beauty in the dust.

A Testament of the Heart's Journey

With every step upon this road,
I carry my burdens, my heavy load.
Yet whispers of love dance through the air,
A testament, a holy prayer.

Through valleys low and mountains high,
In moments of doubt, I reach for the sky.
My heart is the compass, forever seeks
The light that within me quietly speaks.

Each joy and sorrow, a chapter unfolds,
In the silence of night, the truth beholds.
Faith shines brightest when shadows cast,
With grace, I will weave my story vast.

In sacred places, I find my peace,
The heart's journey shall never cease.
For love is the thread that binds us all,
In unity, we rise, together we fall.

So take my hand, when storms arise,
In the solace, our spirits rise.
With every heartbeat, a pledge anew,
A testament of love, forever true.

A Tapestry Woven with Threads of Faith

In the loom of life, we weave our strands,
Colors of hope slip through our hands.
Every prayer is a stitch so fine,
Together they craft a design divine.

From trials faced to joys embraced,
Each moment captured, eternally traced.
In the fabric of love, we find our way,
Guided by the light of each blessed day.

Threads of compassion, entwined with care,
A tapestry rich, beyond compare.
Binding our souls in unity's grace,
With every heartbeat, we honor this space.

Through laughter and tears, joys interlace,
In this sacred art, we find our place.
Faith is the needle, piercing the dark,
Creating a legacy, leaving a mark.

As we walk together, side by side,
In the warmth of love, we shall abide.
With each woven thread, a story to tell,
In the tapestry of faith, all is well.

Unseen Moments of Grace

In the quiet corners of daily life,
Where chaos brews and stirs the strife.
Unseen moments, gently they bloom,
Filling hearts with light, dispelling gloom.

Miracles hidden in the mundane,
A smile, a touch, when joy was feigned.
In details small, God's love replies,
In whispers soft, the spirit flies.

Through trials faced, we learn to see,
The grace that flows, eternally free.
With every heartbeat, a melody plays,
In unseen moments, our spirit sways.

When doubts arise, when paths grow dim,
Hope ignites, our souls will brim.
In stillness, we find the sacred trace,
Of every unseen moment of grace.

Let us tread lightly, embrace the now,
In faith's embrace, we take a vow.
For in the unnoticed, the real treasures lie,
In unseen moments, together we fly.

Milton Keynes UK
Ingram Content Group UK Ltd.
UKHW022223251124
451566UK00006B/104